The National Poetry Series

The National Poetry Series was established in 1978 to ensure the publication of five poetry books annually through five participating publishers. Publication is funded by the Lannan Foundation, Stephen Graham, the Joyce & Seward Johnson Foundation, Glenn and Renee Schaeffer, Juliet Lea Hillman Simonds, and the Edward T. Cone Foundation.

2010 Competition Winners

Lauren Berry of Houston, Texas,
The Lifting Dress
Chosen by Terrance Hayes,
to be published by Penguin Books

William Billiter of Clinton, New York,
Stutter
Chosen by Hilda Raz,
to be published by University of Georgia Press

James Grinwis of Florence, Massachusetts,
Exhibit of Forking Paths
Chosen by Eleni Sikelianos,
to be published by Coffee House Press

M. A. Vizsolyi of New York, New York,
The Lamp with Wings: 60 love sonnets
Chosen by Ilya Kaminsky,
to be published by HarperCollins Publishers

Laura Wetherington of Roanoke, Virginia,
A Map Predetermined and Chance
Chosen by C. S. Giscombe,
to be published by Fence Books

Exhibit of Forking Paths

Exhibit of Forking Paths

POEMS

James Grinwis

COFFEE HOUSE PRESS

MINNEAPOLIS

2011

Coffee House Press books are available to the trade through our primary distributor, Consortium Book Sales & Distribution, www.cbsd.com or (800) 283-3572. For personal orders, catalogs, or other information, write to: info@coffeehousepress.org.

Coffee House Press is a nonprofit literary publishing house. Support from private foundations, corporate giving programs, government programs, and generous individuals helps make the publication of our books possible. We gratefully acknowledge their support in detail in the back of this book.

To you and our many readers around the world,
we send our thanks for your continuing support.

LIBRARY OF CONGRESS CIP INFORMATION
Grinwis, James.
Exhibit of forking paths: poems / by James Grinwis.
p. cm.
ISBN 978-1-56689-280-3 (alk. paper)
I. Title.
2011028636
PRINTED IN THE UNITED STATES
1 3 5 7 9 8 6 4 2
FIRST EDITION | FIRST PRINTING

ACKNOWLEDGMENTS
I am grateful to the editors of the following journals, where some of these poems first appeared, sometimes in slightly different versions: *Colorado Review*: "Landscape Lento"; *Conjunctions*: "Pictures of the Sea," "Format" and *Web Conjunctions*: "Halo with Bolt Through It"; *Crazyhorse*: "Of Phantoms"; *Isotope*: "Earthbound"; *La Petite Zine*: "Exhibit of Forking Paths"; *LIT*: "Arcturus"; *The Literary Review* and *Verse Daily*: "Climograph"; *Lungfull*: "Acknowledgement"; *Modern Review*: "Something that Waves"; *Packingtown Review*: "Condenser," "Chassis Ground"; *Puerto del Sol*: "Man in Umiak with Spear"; *Sawbuck*: "Wisconsonian"; *Segue*: "Bird Sculptures 3"; *Shampoo*: "Inupiat"; *Sentence*: as "Signs of Electricity"—"Capacitor," "Diode," "Light-Emitting Diode," "Thermistor," "Aerial," "Microphone," "Loudspeaker," "NPN Transistor"; *Swerve*: "Canine as a Kind of Tooth," "Format (2)"; *Vallum*: as "Signs of Order in the Universe 3"—"Rheostat," "Variable Inductor," "Duplex Receptacle," "Circuit Breaker."

I am also grateful to the late Agha Shahid Ali, Michael Burkard, James Haug, James Tate, Dara Wier, and the Western MA po-group for inestimable help regarding many of these poems. Thanks also to my friends and family and most of all to Ashley.

for Ashley

One

Two

Three

Four

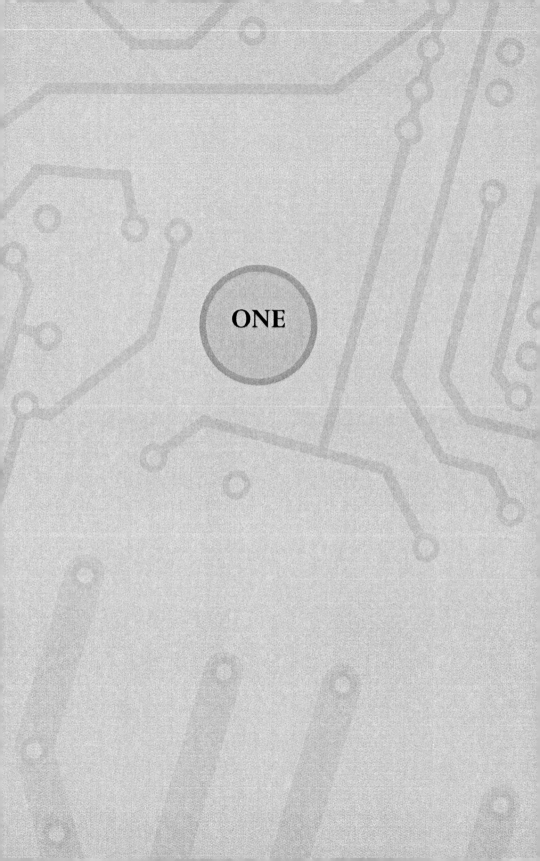

ONE

EXHIBIT OF FORKING PATHS

In tablet 1 2 is a girl in ski boots
wading a lushly gurgling stream.

I am defeated.
In tablet 4, an ex–torture chamber attendant
shucks the shells of shrimps
and crawfish. He is opening
a bar, "The Shuck." A nosy insect
screams in a tree behind him.

Tablet 2 2 2: Mr. R., digging
a small pit for a vial of barbiturates.
The hair on his back is long and fuzzy.

The end of love. A tall sundial.
A genie strangled and left on the curb
like a derelict's rag.

I am torn. Wasted.
A pummeled plate. A dent.

Tablet 1 6 hangs from an ambiguous
ceiling fixture. The coronary form
or a used tea bag smelling of olive juice.
An ear, perhaps a dog's,
folded over a medium-sized clamshell.
A used bandage also.

In the igneous tree,
I stuck the remains.
My ego slithered off
like a horned lizard into the bubbly mud.

In tablet 70, a walrus. A severed walrus
head. A tusk half-yanked
and jerking under the Floridian wind.
There is a black sun in the scene.

In tablet 71, a snore personified.
It scuttles around as befits
a defeathered hen, a large rock
falling on top of it.

Defeat, failure worming around,
gored, swamped by a conglomerate of waves
and chieftains riding the waves
on smooth sealskin tubs.

Tablet 420 strikes the observer
with its direct attention to the suffering
of abandoned dogs, and the crippled boys
and the bleeding-to-death civilians who find them.

Tablet 5, propped on the picaresque nightstand,
consists of the fragments of smashed cassette tapes
and shattered compact discs.
They are arranged in such a way
as to resemble the luminous crystals
that burst from the rock on tall mountains

or at the bottom of seas.
A cord extends to an outlet that,
when plugged in, illuminates the tablet
like the scales of a tuna or tweaked moonlight
on the Pacific Rim.

Adi loves tablet 637: of the minstrel of cotton
and wine stirring a wineglass with fingers of needles and stems.
I drink too much, she thinks.

Of tablet 91, the residents
of the care facility agree: it's too fruity.

In the care of the critics of scalpel gaze,
an unnumbered tablet has been whisked.
It is a void of few feathers
and a cardboard nose.

In the case of tablet 31, we will not speak.
A boy is alternately blowing his nose
and ringing a doorbell shrilly.

Capacitor
(stores charge)
and **Variable Capacitor**
(stores varying amounts of charge)

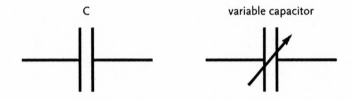

On the way to the store a delivery truck collided into a wall, behind which a group of men were throwing javelins, many of which had thocked into the truck-rammed wall with the violence spilling out of the throwers' hearts.

*

On the way to the arcade a truck carrying a fake mummy skidded on some spilled iguana skins and veered sharply just shy of a wall behind which a woman was wringing a great blue cloth with a creaking winch and much of the dye is splattering onto the concrete floor along with the water, though the woman is considering letting go of the winch handle and watching everything unspool.

Diode

(permits current to flow in one direction only;
can also be used to convert ac signals to dc signals [a "rectifier"])

We are all of us gathered here today to witness the joining of two lovers, one of which is a bit larger and more lusty than the other, when a boy on a moped screeches into the gathering like a blasted organ pipe, upsetting the bride and crashing through the huge Achilles shield the groom has withdrawn. The bride turns against the man she was about to join in holy matrimony, realizing the whole thing was wrong in the first place and could have been avoided. The smoke and dust that had risen into a mushroom cloud calmly descends again like a peaceful yet debilitating ash.

Light-Emitting Diode

(emits light when current flows through it)

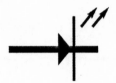

After lassoing the hawk, hauling it down, twisting fireweed about its ankles and setting it free, after the bonfire had dwindled down and the last of the sirloin had been eaten, the barbecue sauce rubbed into their jeans, Tina and Sam spread a bearskin over the outcrop that overlooked Diamond Lake, the moonlight streaming and the stars straining, everything seemingly happy with everything else, Buddhistic almost, with the diatoms on the pond buzzing out luminescence like the selfsame elements comprising the lake's name, and fucked each other silly.

Thermistor

(converts temperature variations into resistence)

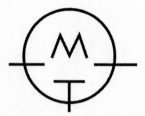

In my little chopped hat, my mask and club, nothing escapes me. A ray slices through and is thoroughly cut up and absorbed like a wolf in a mud paddy or like a man obsessed with tiny books and pocket encyclopedias running into an oversized library. An alligator has closed its jaws over a cluster of fat chickens. Thunder, tyrannosaurs, trephination; no, it's about entering a sphere and being spun about, shot up, shot down, flushed down a drain to emerge in one piece so wet, so new.

Aerial

(converts radio waves in ac signals and vice versa)

The cannibal's charm. Go ahead, it says. You're young, excite me. Three tall fires were puncturing the darkness. They shot out from the tip of an icicle. A trifecta-ed lion. An old man slides down a mountain, his legs splayed to the side. An old man wielding the leg of an extinct bird, shouting "Quack Quack!"

Microphone

(converts sound waves into ac voltage)

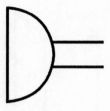

Two spikes were rammed into the ovoid door of a cave. Behind that door was another door, a flat one. Behind that, who knew.

Loudspeaker

(converts ac signals into sound waves)

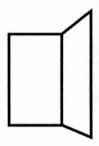

Flat box shapes rule the land of lost totems.

NPN Transistor

(amplifies electric current and turns it on or off)

and **PNP Transistor**

(amplifies electric current and turns it off or on)

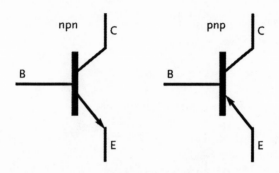

A boy has entered a region of meditation, landscaped with elegant grasses, sleek, lunar stones, and thrashes around in it. A state of confusion, very lost and unusually shaped.

*

A small furnace has broken and a young fire has broken out in a health care facility. Oxygen rushes in like a funneled spear. The era for sailing ships is no longer a ballad but a swift march to the sea. A man in a green robe looks like a prism of filtered fright. He dumps water on the fire, a single pail, and shoots into his fate. It is an electrical fire and no one in sight can stop it. Until much later along in the unhurried day.

PICTURES OF THE SEA

Scuba diver with crystalline utensil.

Scuba diver of flagrant gear
using a small shovel to scoop up sand.

Octopus clasping discarded propeller.

Portrait of blanket with ice in background.

Background with toenail exposed.

Snake shape. More than enough of holes.

Cult of the box:

They had put down their cell phones and were gathered around, tucked inside their frog suits. The box yawned open like a great yellowing shrubbery. The hands of the clock spun too slowly for us secreted observers, staring out from our camouflaged barriers. My eyes felt like overflowing beakers, so I badly wanted to know what was inside. I dialed the base but was told nothing. The light was getting thick. Far away, someone was practicing a Bach concerto on a squeaky viola. And a cluster of salt shakers was dangling on elastic cords hanging down from the darkened stage. My fingers were all twiddled out. I kept thinking it was time to make our move but directions were forthcoming and nobody on the team seemed very excited anyway.

Nurse shark embedded in salt weed.

Pemmican fish.

Tough, old dog, torn from his drifting scrap of wood.

PICTURES OF SPACE

Shackleton, retired, shelters under an elm tree during a light
Shropshire rain.

The nitty-gritty gleamed: little or no thought seemed exemplary.

Starting to walk again, the freezing people after the storm.
Huge tanks dotting the tundra: glass cubes implicated.

Isamu Noguchi in pursuit of chance
coaxes sled dogs forward.

Staring contest going on in the hold of the steamship;
it lasts all night, like it was with Teresa and the sailors. There is a blinking
on the outskirts of the scene.

Abraham Ortelius was a Flemish cartographer. He drank sangria
              in the manner
of a brilliant cartographer, New Mexico, circa 1566.

A mixing of setting and time occurred.
Very green out, humid, and arctic.
Aesthetic as image jumbling. Aesthetic as elegant,
bone-gnawed landscape. Unfinished done business.

We had been looking through large open windows to glimpse the secrets
of presumably herpetologist-inclined rooms. The team members
continued to slip off for coffee and glimpses of algae-coated stories. The

stars appeared to be imminent, and a number of irregular desk components had turned to little humans and poured into the Soho streets. In order to be made aware of the architectural catastrophes taking root across the project, Luke murmured into the device.

Nuuk: a new island in Dubai. Flagrant: a kind of foul.

Waterfowl were littering the urban pond. The rats
at night: small, carnivorous attempts.

The aesthetic: doomed. A broken style, its wings pulled out.
A damaged refrigerator with anorexic breasts pressed against it.

You are quiet.

BIRD SCULPTURES 3

Half-Bird Half-Dromedary
Bird Flash Unit
Thinking Bird
Circuit of Clothes Birds
Bird with Sponge for Face
Bird Made of 3 Twisted Leaves
Bird of Her Hair Descends to Snip Me
Loose, Apocalyptic Bird Pecking Bucket of Polymers
Bird with Harvest Moon, 1960
Bird as Serrated Edge
Bird with Igloo for Beak
Bird Jammed in Wall
Bird Caught and Rammed into Stereo Speaker
Night Hawk Tearing Lawn Sprinkler to Shreds
Scissor Bird
Avalanche Bird
Bird Made of Foil, Saran Wrap, and Shells
Bird Made of Paste
Wooden Louse Bird
Bird with Wire Frame
Planted Bird
The Bird Ship
Bird off Highway 9, Spring, 1972
Cave Bird
Ice Bird with Suckling Pig
In the Land of Harvested Birds
The Non-Bird

Bird Made of Alternating Magnetic Bits
Bird Made of Escalator Cable
Bird Made of Escalator Pads
Bird Suspended by 3 Wires
Bird Mounted on Fossilized Vegetable
Bird Floating in Chowder
Bolted Bird with Flexed Talon
Soft Shell Bird
I curled my fingers over the bird, it swelled and strained for night
Heavy was the heart of the bird and light

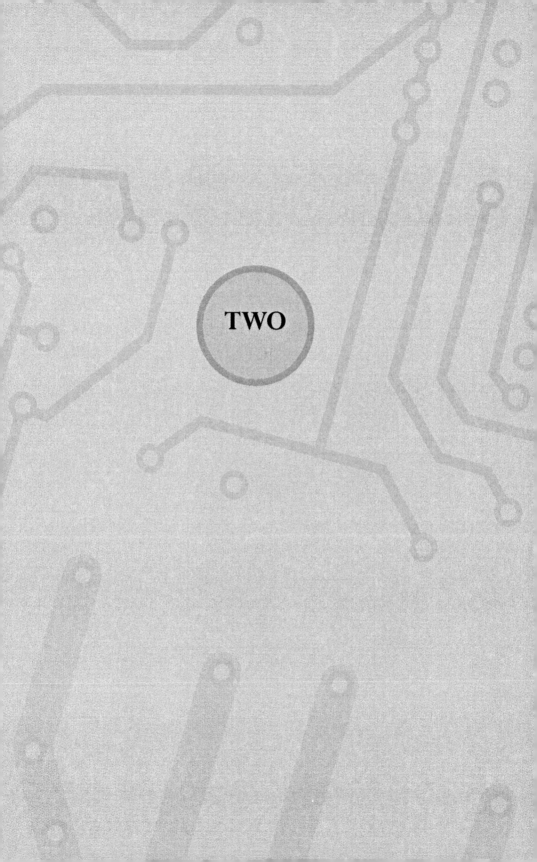

TWO

CANINE AS A KIND OF TOOTH

Fine tuning. Fire twig.
The chip shop. Sizzling types
of vegetable oils. Fries, clams,
hot sauce. In the corner booth,
a boy digs his claws in deeply,
the girl he's with grins.
Boys dig, girls make nets:
a fallacy or not.
Taciturn. Bloodhound-less.
Hope all's well with you.

*

Oversexed. Under
weather. Some say a microchip
embedded by an alien
is at the root of us.
A trainer of whippets,
a whippet-eer. Nobody being
nobody, she whispers
under her brainstorm.
A cube of fat. Passion
all used up.

*

Far afield. The nowhere
lined road. Empty warehouses.
Shrimp shacks abandoned
like spools of twine. A man
driving up and down
chased by terriers.
Once he was a champion
and so were the terriers.
A Welsh, a Boston,
and a Yorkie. On the way
to a landscape dotted
with trees and restaurants.
On the way to a land of beaches
to grind something.

*

Sorrowful bundles. A man
full of magazines. Time for,
placement against. No way
to run faster and better.
A pack of pugs stampeding
over the plain. I can't stand to see
anybody cry even very
young children. My thumbs
lengthen, been reading
all day. Testament to non-talk.
Falling flat, the recent discovery.
And the sea's green shake.

*

At which moment and what direction
comes the hurrah. Wrecked.
Lifting up. Need to crush
egoism and things. To fall apart
with a smile. For all time.
Look: a dachshund tearing
a billy goat to shreds. And a llama
sticking its tongue out
from a topmost branch.

ACKNOWLEDGMENT

Ghost made of glass

ghost made of brick and smashed birds

ghost of raindrops

of silkweed and lint

ghost of the stumps of beech trees

the fallen limbs of pine

that ghost of scrabble chips

of the holes of woodpeckers

there is the ghost of Fridays and Sundays

in March or June the smoke of small

fires deep in the woods,

the ghosts of burning airshafts

the mermaids of castoff myths

a glue stick of a ghost

an area beyond ghostliness

is it the stealth ghost

the one who stares while he moves

eats the legs of gazelles while she sleeps.

OF PHANTOMS

even a phantom gets thirsty
—KAZUKO SHIRAISHI

And you must take care of your phantom.
He is like a bird,

fragile, grounded.

But featherless. Like a baby's head,

fuzzy.

His face like a tooth blasted apart, though;
only a spike would mess with it.

Still, he is your phantom. Care for him.

We must care for the things under our wings
and auspices.

Even if they are gawky, and have odd
manners and styles

like those with roots in places
through which they but wander.

Condenser

(stores charge) [symbol obsolete: see *Capacitor*]

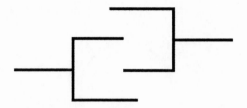

Four vehicles have taken off from parallel locations and soon pair off toward an emptiness characterized by large white spaces unless, in actuality, two pairs of vehicles as they approach one another diverge and split off into parallel lonelinesses where the white spaces are more controlled, managed even, by some vague force akin to a child simultaneously spinning a top and firing his slingshot while at the same time seeing, on the surface of the pond, the plunk of water caused by the stone and the hollow spot on the deck where the top has ground its nub and then found rest.

Armature

(carries current, generates force)

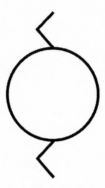

Two shearwaters, after Tina and Jim have hauled them down with nets then released them with blue hair ribbons tied to their legs, begin to circle in a kind of love duet so fierce but smooth that, in the mythology of seabirds, they become symbolic of the tyrannosaur and tyrannosauress shaking the earth in fits of necessary rage to give birth. Their circular dance finds the grace to contain for a moment the typhoon hiding in the infinitesimal silence of the core, while Joey waits for its gusty, springlike release.

Chassis Ground

(point of zero voltage: all currents measured by it)

And in the beginning was the force and the need for force and the hazy fuel outages in the sun, and in the end was a toppled radiator, a single fence post casting three sad shadows, the business end of an old gardening utensil that a lover of de Chirico wields in strange attempts to live like de Chirico, hoping to wed a Russian ballerina, and paint, and have one of his paintings grace the cover of an album by Thelonious Monk, and paint, and make of a single afternoon an enigma, an inhabited space a giant sparseness, and have a brother named Albert.

Blowout

(produces magnetic field, lengthens and extinguishes arc)

In the baby was a darkness and in the eye of the baby a constant pulse of "no" beaten in the form of a snake with two heads trying to run away with the snake in opposite directions. Laura came into the room made of alternating corners and the eyes of the fishermen riveted themselves on the twin helms of her hip posts and on the base of her spine where doubleness is honed into the best vessel any man had known. Also in the scene: a boy peeing while lifting one leg to keep an infant or a dog from getting inside the stream.

Potentiometer
(variable resistor, divides charge, measures voltage)

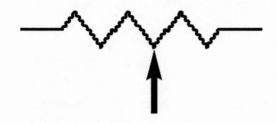

Look, there is a path through a safe, clear space into a kind of deep woods, the way a late romantic is woods, an "ordered" woods: hacked up trees, gross vines, but there can be found trolleys, and power saws in the distance erecting a sound house for extinct songbirds, because there are directions that are always clearly *toward* and those that suggest always *from,* which is how one may go inward to fix the rough spots the way a blood cell endeavors to surround a disease, drinking a squeeze of lemon, watching a woman who reminds one of one's lost love or wife or someone who is otherwise no longer reachable though yearned for to the extent that any woman may resemble her, watching as she goes back and forth between the customers in a place where, every night, there is a transition from deep quiet, as found in snow, to a more static form, as found in heat, while Helsinki and surfboards and places that will not be seen linger in the background.

Before the snowfall, there was a dog nosing around some weeds at the side of the road, and a kid in a car is coming, and the kid, exhibiting euphoria for the fuel pedal in celebration of his winning an entry-level position at Charles Schwab or Merrill Lynch, though my gripe is with the kid for killing the dog not with Merrill Lynch for giving him the job, a fine company, and its logo, Merrill Lynch's, is really great:

a bull or a water buffalo who looks kind of like the dog did when standing tall, sighting something in the woods, maybe it was the woman he sighted, the one on the plane who resembled my wife, she had her computer open to a document about Merrill Lynch and Brazil or was it Hartford, the jungle has gotten thicker, more buggy, there could be some Williamses here, maybe Vaughan, Venus, and William Carlos here looking at one another with the polite respect we share for those we think we like and are curious about, stepping back, giving them room, hesitating before asking anything.

Something about how force pumps down, pushes itself, from beauty to jaggedness and vice versa, the way the baby is tearing up some papers, important papers though they look small in his tiny, crushing hands.

AWRY

Because I am born,
I feel things about
not being.
Because there are five planets
holding themselves
against a huge, bleached face,
I write things.
Like "hello" and
"I know you from somewhere."
I am consistently
alone and don't spend time cooking.
An aardvark trailed
her tail over my last appreciation
of Bach's fourth cello suite
but I was too far away
to catch it.
An aardvark is a shy beast
but is also called ant bear
and can fend off wildcats
with its lacerating claws.
An aardwolf is also
quite shy and delicate
but has neither fierce claws
or tubed teeth, preferring
sturdier teeth.
A sportive lemur
looks at me

because I disappear.
Much the way I did
when I pulled out of a house
and saw a gaze that was
a heart-shaped tooth.
I pull out of a lot of things
these days. Mighty good chowder
fizzling on the burner.
Notes will burrow
in forms that remain
somewhat unknown.

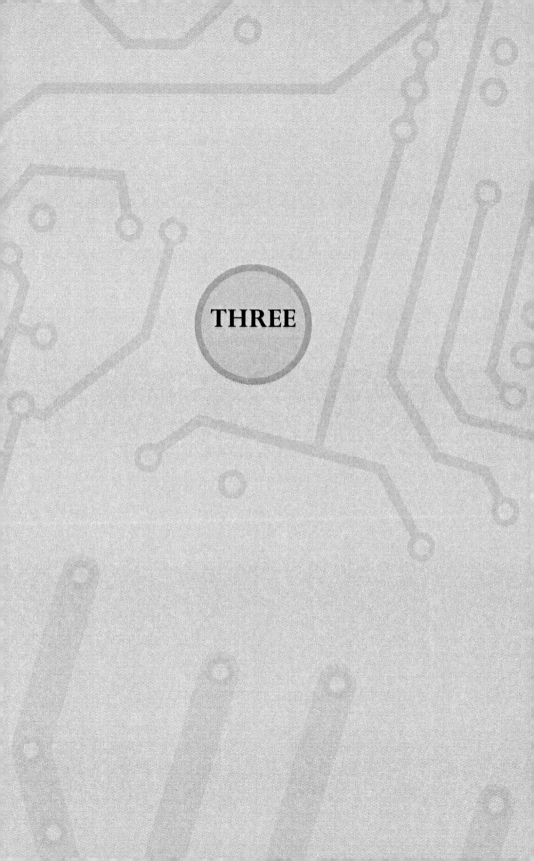

THREE

INUPIAT

Stinkfish. Seal flipper.
What have you

north of you.
Beside someone's margin loss,

a whale basking
like a spring tripped

in some kind of mechanical accident
between naturalized service devices.

Not to say
things are normal or at all close

to those who run
kinless across the fields,

flicking the last drops of sun from the sky.
Though, while in transit,

things glitter.

FORMAT

An ibis made of whalebone.
A dart made of glass.
A glow as from an office at night
emanating from a smooth orb
you can place anywhere.
A photograph of the tundra,
a little hut surrounded
by wolves. A man at the door
throwing slabs of bread
to the wolves. A photograph
of the tropics, an equatorial
stream. A woman in a square boat
tossing strips of meat
to swans. A campfire.
Gathering stones to line
the fire, sticks. The arms of the fire
like the wings of a harp-eagle.
The eagle like the sound
of a missing train. A box.
A small white box
from Korea or Japan
that looks like an inflated envelope.
To not open the box,
to just stare at it
for a great length of time.
A monk pushing a bamboo rake
across a field of small stones.

A bigger stone
inside the smaller one.
A cloud empty of another cloud.
A tree.

LANDSCAPE LENTO

I think in terms of landscape.

Look, there is a little man resembling Kenneth Branagh
walking across the landscape.

A soprano-sized wind nips down. Kenneth's coat
looks like it's sewn from breadcrumbs. It exudes
an odor of pine flakes.

There's no ice palace, but a little wood / adobe hut,
a stovepipe poking out and pumping a curdle of smoke.

A man, it looks like Calvin Trillin, uncorks a window
and inhales a batch of the bitter air.

Nothing comes easy. The soul stares at its image in the ghost mirror.
A lantern glows vastly across the ghost mirror, which releases an
eerie whine backed by a far-off organ grinder. There is an inter-
mezzo that creates itself and weaves its notes only for you, a
mingling of winds inside: the wind's own ghost mirror:

Snow. Idea of snow. Sounds of the stuff.

A small, happy boy on a bench beside a new fire gorges himself
on steamed dumplings.

His older brother, breath coming out in fierce blasts,
chews on a packet of soy sauce that explodes and sends it spewing
down his chin to make a black stain in the snow.

Several luminosities there are no names for.

I will return to Morocco tomorrow.

Rheostat
(variable resistor, handles high current)

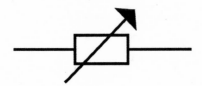

Miles woke up and it was around two a.m. He picked up his cell to call her and he got the voice message again so hung up. He felt very alone, more than usual, and put himself down and lit a small bonfire in the center of his room. A spark shot out into the air like an Aztec charm and illuminated the space where emptiness was a bundle of strings and an animal appeared to swing upon them.

Variable Inductor

(varies value over a given range)

L   variable inductor

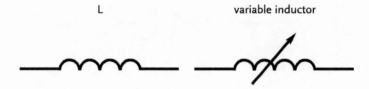

If you are being in this box then this box fits, if you are looking at your feet from your space in the box then your feet are very smooth and not of this box, though you want to move a little, so you move in the manner of someone unbeknownst to movement.

You do and the weight you carry with you shifts. It is odd, this weight, like you were driving a large and ungainly vehicle through the vehicle, and at the moment of shifting, it grows boneless, light enough to move.

Snap Switch

(springs under tension, joins currents)

The arrows have struck one another, and the people are pulling them apart. When he goes to the office, his tie never fits. Then she whose belt is too large comes to him.

Blowout #2

(creates magnetic field, destroys arc)

From point to point there is no direct route for the animals. A shark has plunged into her own tail meanwhile. A fork whose tines have been pried apart pokes from a treeless ground. The actors in a stage play get naked and rip meaning from the sheath the playwright has made, hence.

Tiepoint
(distributes charge)

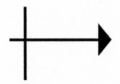

When he rounds the corner it is she who has come into his bank and upset the postmen, or there are others not known to them who spit fried, drenched squid onto the crosswalk as they cross themselves with branches of dead pines in order to seem at one with the woodlands, and the vehicular osmosis of the landscape presents a kind of bed to him, and she decides from a vague point in her mind to discern what is indiscernible and better left for the one winged vulture who begs for any kind of scrap you can give, and does not leap into the bed he has made, just stares at it, and he removes the old blade from the lump, which creaks and sounds sweet.

Shielded Wire
(protects charge, limits electromagnetic flow)

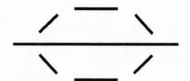

There is the crevasse splitting the white landscape, and six research laboratories, clustered around the abyss, study the properties of the holes. During their cigarette breaks, the scientists look at each other across the way from behind the long windows, wondering who is getting lucky, and how many nights would they need.

Singleplex Receptacle

(provides point in system where current can be
taken to run devices x 1)

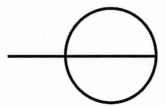

There are several aspects to the dimension that is both a taking in and a taking out of a zone that is both zoneless and entirely at home. Snow billows inside the crest of a deep fish, a skewed arrangement between ghosts. There are spikes that are meant to strike and those meant to be hidden and remain untouched.

Duplex Receptacle

(provides point in system where current can be
taken to run devices x 2)

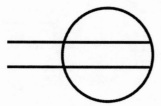

There are areas of pointedness and unpointedness though here at least is a beast with nothing between his beak but infinite space, an artful beast who has imagined a cadaver and placed its yellowing form in Sheila's white-toed universe box. Often are little faces in the walls and you may not touch them but watch them.

Synchro

(measures angle of rotating machines)

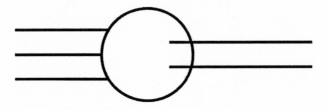

Three vehicles have taken themselves from the place and blasted away to the west, and two secreted ones have shot for the east, in search of supplies for the impregnations going on day after day in the inner sanctum while the outer sanctum holds splendid little cafés and utilities for the males to amuse themselves with when not being amused by the peacemaker who lives in two large huts whose doors face the inside and the outside respectively, the peacemaker who decides who should lie with whom and how such-and-such an individual should be measured, and respond thereof.

Wall-Mounted Light Fixture

(reduces glare)

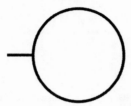

He is looking that way and his nose is long and sharp and he is the
mystery man of great and large ideas cast in gently muted tones.
There is a spilled crane in the scene.

Circuit Breaker
(activates or deactivates path of charge)

We are gathered here to witness a small hill in the ground. There is a sundown, and the day has some dregs left in it. Wait for me, the great one said.

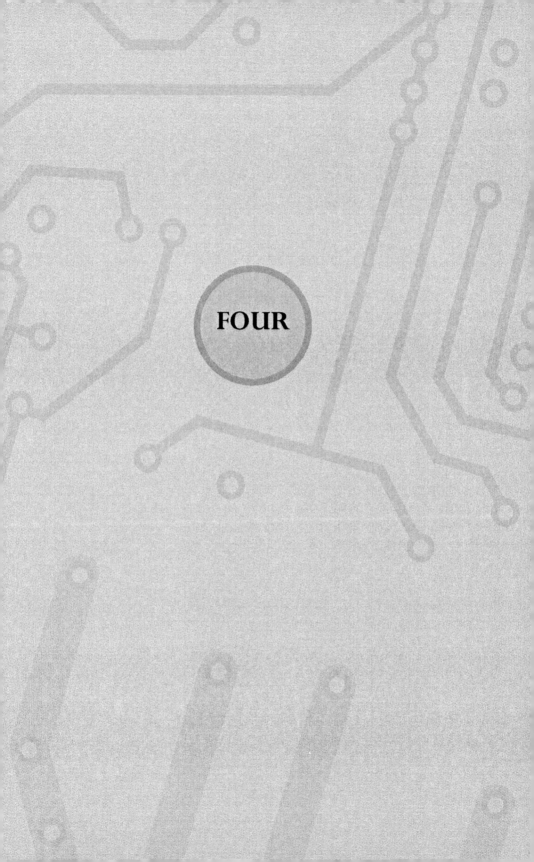

FOUR

SOMETHING THAT WAVES

Argyll forest.
Landscape of toenails.

The perpetually shoeless walk around
waiting for something to happen.

There are Argyll wolves and Argyll antelopes
and cavemen. The soups were simmering in the tubs.

Like a giant crane that no longer worked,
the visions next. Vacant, monolithic spaces.

It will get extremely hot, she will be sensual
and show you her beautiful fingers.

Versions of glory: hold onto a thing that moves.

Fountains and fires occupied the terraces,
Argyll geckos and newts studding the crenellations
and roofs of the town.

An infatuation with lazing around
watered the businesses, schools, and bus terminals.

An infatuation with states of being not being.

ARCTURUS

or Glowworms and Other Heights of Awareness.

To see better, we do not stare directly at objects at night,
the eyes focus on the edges of things.

Hot spots are full of rods. This thing of terms:
what the sounds mean before the definitions of sounds.

Like a glass robe, or a spirit
weighted down with bunnies who have too often
eaten many nickels.

All of the discarded and forgotten pennies in the world
congealed into a hideous red form, the revenge of the poor
descending on overblown enterprises

with the silvery wings of a Cronos reborn from mud and fire
to roam and lay waste.

I come to the field and aim a telescope
at a common occurrence of Messier's tome,
the ghost of Olivier Messiaen coaxing fireflies from their dens

to make a shroud of inconstant light.

FORMAT (2)

A missing lounge chair.
A yellow chair around which are scattered
enormous certificates made out to x.
A sound husked,
hanging in the air like a stone.
The room as being inside
of a stone.
A bag. A bag of illuminated
things, like lactiferous ducts
glowing inside of a breast.
A hatchling. A hatchling holding
a nose ring in its mouth.
A portrait of a diabolical entity
where the heart may remain usurped
in indeterminate space.
A fuse. A fuse snagged between pincers
and fizzing.
A tumbler of gin,
a cup where the ice
knocks the sides of the glass
the way canoes bump the sides of a dock.
Light, but little of it.
Light as encased in a jar
sealed in a mineshaft.
That which comes last
holding out in a mineshaft
in wait for what is.

MAN IN UMIAK WITH SPEAR

Poem head. War
canoe. Edge of the last
leaf. Edge of the snowblower
bobbing in the surf.
No privacy here,
with a nomad and a nomad's
dog, devouring a peanut butter
and honey sandwich.
Farmchild. City kid.
Nobody home
in the blankness.
Two figures in a single
shaft of stone
meld as if violence
consisted of one fluid strip.
In the country of beached whales,
a voice like a syrup tendril
clinging to an antler.
Still, a girl laughed
in the parlor at the end
of the strip. Maybe
it is violent,
technical.

Halo with Bolt Through It

(creates slants of current, alters behavioral traits)

In the overture a finch caresses a watermelon with its beak. It is a large watermelon and the bird is very small. You are reminded of several images but one or another stands out. In the space where the oboe hesitates under the press of strings a mistress rubs ointment into her throat, or perhaps it is blood from the blood vial. Many dots coalesce and crawl together or make very small holes in space.

Flat Space with Series of Arcs
(generates confusion, redirects charge)

At the drawing table are pulled up representatives of ambition both crushed and realized. A pineapple cracked open is at the center of the table and what protrudes from it is a miniature video camera. In the lens of the camera, an ensemble realizes a suite for piano and five trombones. It is hairy outside, white hair strands filling the air and people are writhing on the street, retching. In a storefront window a young man is eating lemon meringue off the ample, gleaming ass of his cocktail waitress, and everywhere the lonely cling to loss sculptures.

Boomerang in Void Shape
(maintains pressure, relates atmosphere and alters course)

Two attractive and adventurous women appeared and wanted to talk but he was drinking, and because his friend had left he was alone and drinking, and the last thing he saw before he made his stumble home was the serpent with the moth in its beak peering from the panty line at her spine. He never would have thought that this would take hold in his memory and live on like a banshee of what might have been, like a hoop dropping through a hoop-carrying circus performer to settle in the midst of a mini extinction. Or what it might not have been.

Blob Shapes Floating Downstream

(probes reason and current)

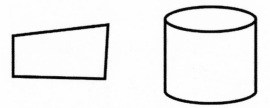

In the dissection of the circle the hostess was unclear: to remove the un-guts before the spinal column or take the femur and align it with the skull? There is memory within the non-memory like a roadster envisioning the spaceship that has come to move us in a suppler and more malleable direction.

Fuse

(breaks current, beats overloads)

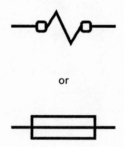

or

To forget and then to remember. It was a ladder, fading. A kid with truckloads of belief, to have something important to do and evaporate into the strange windows. To push open a window to leave something behind.

WISCONSONIAN

Looking for Sibelius's bicycle.

The squares of a Moroccan rug came undone
surrounded by estrogen

Replicas, frameworks, strings

Movement like billboards,
scissors pulled from sacs.

A young woman came
pulling herself as an extraction of hair
from mole ears.

People, hunting the tempests inside them
with barbed shots of beer.

I was left to convey pieces.

He had, Sibelius, it is believed,

a number of bicycles.

*

A geography of low hair.

Explosions like peanuts.

An inverted "I."

Oats like corks.

Hidden boxcar cities.

I decided to call before sensing it.

Ego as gel, solidifying, oat-like

Morrisons

Good magic for bad, tap the wand
one times forward two times.

*

The hills are past the shapes of

not being what I've since become, to nestle deeper.

Clouds like sacs of charcoal.

Slightly Mephistophelian, the clouds.

Most everyone bitching

you spit a pit into your palm
and place it back into your mouth

the world for this

seems to come together of sorts.

CLIMOGRAPH

To be a valley inside walls.
To be revealed in nothing.
A bathtub floating.
A squid like a mess of bulbous lice.
The bubbles in the tub, the slab
of soap, the oat boy
hanging down from the cloud.
Untied, noticing what moves.

*

What is seen in the motion
and what is felt.
A formula for flight
bubbling over to hiss
against the windows of paradise
and the windows of those places
better left dark.
To be a quill trailing
out of a gored muskrat.
To be the circle inside
a swan dive, a node buzzing
through an unsung state.

*

The beyond goes only as far
as ourselves, she said.
The ocean seemed pummeled
with girls' fists.
A general understanding of earth
made the windows of the apartment
glow and radiate a series of hums.
To be a wind funnel bent.
A cup of something strong
on the desk of an innocent.
A downpour caught
in a carton of flowers.

EARTHBOUND

Big sky flexion,
a guess. I unfold
my map. Here is Aldebaran
here is Polaris. Little crevices
slicing the moon. Walking far,
the corrosive light.
To the left, an odd species
of tree, feeding on dawn.

*

Earth at night
reveals things we
diurnal folks wouldn't believe.
Love's enough though.
What was it the great man said:
I have walked too long for death.

*

Oddball nebula,
nefarious smooch.
In the land of the very-hot-pepper eaters,
moonshine tastes sweet.
Pack your passport, your cutlery kit,
a little sense of your own unknown.
Odor of crushed fleas,

sound of one horn
in a field of mice.
Sweep me, the frail dust mite said.
Star flesh isn't rotten,
but covered in lice.

*

Two micron all-sky survey.
From Amherst to spaceland
the scholar of Aztec calendars
flew. Something about rain,
the thick scent of it,
like moist smoke.

COLOPHON

Exhibit of Forking Paths was designed at Coffee House Press, in the historic
Grain Belt Brewery's Bottling House near downtown Minneapolis.
The text is set in Perpetua.

FUNDER ACKNOWLEDGMENT

Coffee House Press is an independent nonprofit literary publisher. Our books are made possible through the generous support of grants and gifts from many foundations, corporate giving programs, state and federal support, and through donations from individuals who believe in the transformational power of literature. Coffee House Press receives major operating support from the Bush Foundation, the McKnight Foundation, from Target, and from the Minnesota State Arts Board, through an appropriation from the Minnesota State Legislature and from the National Endowment for the Arts. Coffee House also receives support from: three anonymous donors; Elmer L. and Eleanor J. Andersen Foundation; Around Town Literary Media Guides; Patricia Beithon; Bill Berkson; the James L. and Nancy J. Bildner Foundation; the E. Thomas Binger and Rebecca Rand Fund of the Minneapolis Foundation; the Patrick and Aimee Butler Family Foundation; the Buuck Family Foundation; Ruth and Bruce Dayton; Dorsey & Whitney, LLP; Mary Ebert and Paul Stembler; Fredrikson & Byron, P.A.; Sally French; Jennifer Haugh; Anselm Hollo and Jane Dalrymple-Hollo; Jeffrey Hom; Stephen and Isabel Keating; the Kenneth Koch Literary Estate; the Lenfestey Family Foundation; Ethan J. Litman; Mary McDermid; Sjur Midness and Briar Andresen; the Rehael Fund of the Minneapolis Foundation; Deborah Reynolds; Schwegman, Lundberg & Woessner, P.A.; John Sjoberg; David Smith; Mary Strand and Tom Fraser; Jeffrey Sugerman; Patricia Tilton; the Archie D. & Bertha H. Walker Foundation; Stu Wilson and Mel Barker; the Woessner Freeman Family Foundation; and many other generous individual donors.

NATIONAL
ENDOWMENT
FOR THE ARTS

This activity is made possible in part by a grant from the Minnesota State Arts Board, through an appropriation by the Minnesota State Legislature and a grant from the National Endowment for the Arts. MINNESOTA STATE ARTS BOARD

TARGET.

To you and our many readers across the country,
we send our thanks for your continuing support.

Good books are brewing at www.coffeehousepress.org